Plan a Week of Meals!

Save Money!

Meal Planner Journal

Activinotes

Activinotes

DAILY JOURNALS, PLANNERS, NOTEBOOKS AND OTHER BLANK BOOKS

Copyright 2016

Love
yourself
enough to
live a healthy
lifestyle

here's to...
BETTER HABITS
positive thinking
CLEAN EATING
& most of all

Loving
Yourself.

Weekly Meal Planner

Day	Breakfast	Lunch	Dinner
Monday			
Tuesday			
Wednesday			
Thursday			
Friday			
Saturday			
Sunday			

Notes

Weekly Meal Planner

things to do

_____
_____
_____
_____
_____
_____
_____

I want healthy dessert

things to buy

_____
_____
_____
_____
_____
_____
_____

List your healthy snacks here . . .

-
-
-
-
-
-
-

Healthy drinks for this week

-
-
-
-

Notes

Weekly Meal Planner

Day	Breakfast	Lunch	Dinner
Monday			
Tuesday			
Wednesday			
Thursday			
Friday			
Saturday			
Sunday			

Notes

Weekly Meal Planner

things to do

_____

_____

_____

_____

_____

_____

_____

I want healthy dessert

things to buy

_____

_____

_____

_____

_____

_____

_____

List your healthy snacks here . . .

-
-
-
-
-
-
-

Healthy drinks for this week

-
-
-
-

Notes

Weekly Meal Planner

Day	Breakfast	Lunch	Dinner
Monday			
Tuesday			
Wednesday			
Thursday			
Friday			
Saturday			
Sunday			

Notes

Weekly Meal Planner

things to do

_____

_____

_____

_____

_____

_____

_____

I want healthy dessert

things to buy

_____

_____

_____

_____

_____

_____

_____

List your healthy snacks here . . .

-
-
-
-
-
-
-

Healthy drinks for this week

-
-
-
-

Notes

Weekly Meal Planner

Day	Breakfast	Lunch	Dinner
Monday			
Tuesday			
Wednesday			
Thursday			
Friday			
Saturday			
Sunday			

Notes

Weekly Meal Planner

things to do

_____

_____

_____

_____

_____

_____

_____

I want healthy dessert

things to buy

_____

_____

_____

_____

_____

_____

_____

List your healthy snacks here . . .

-
-
-
-
-
-
-

Healthy drinks for this week

-
-
-
-

Notes

Weekly Meal Planner

Day	Breakfast	Lunch	Dinner
Monday			
Tuesday			
Wednesday			
Thursday			
Friday			
Saturday			
Sunday			

Notes

Weekly Meal Planner

things to do

_____

_____

_____

_____

_____

_____

I want healthy dessert

things to buy

_____

_____

_____

_____

_____

_____

List your healthy snacks here . . .

-
-
-
-
-
-

Healthy drinks for this week

-
-
-
-

Notes

Weekly Meal Planner

Day	Breakfast	Lunch	Dinner
Monday			
Tuesday			
Wednesday			
Thursday			
Friday			
Saturday			
Sunday			

Notes

Weekly Meal Planner

things to do

_____

_____

_____

_____

_____

_____

_____

I want healthy dessert

things to buy

_____

_____

_____

_____

_____

_____

_____

List your healthy snacks here . . .

-
-
-
-
-
-
-

Healthy drinks for this week

-
-
-
-

Notes

Weekly Meal Planner

Day	Breakfast	Lunch	Dinner
Monday			
Tuesday			
Wednesday			
Thursday			
Friday			
Saturday			
Sunday			

Notes

Weekly Meal Planner

things to do

I want healthy dessert

_____

_____

_____

_____

_____

_____

_____

things to buy

List your healthy snacks here . . .

_____

_____

_____

_____

_____

_____

_____

Healthy drinks for this week

-
-
-
-

-
-
-
-
-
-

Notes

Weekly Meal Planner

Day	Breakfast	Lunch	Dinner
Monday			
Tuesday			
Wednesday			
Thursday			
Friday			
Saturday			
Sunday			

Notes

Weekly Meal Planner

things to do

_____
_____
_____
_____
_____
_____

I want healthy dessert

things to buy

_____
_____
_____
_____
_____
_____

List your healthy snacks here . . .

-
-
-
-
-
-
-

Healthy drinks for this week

-
-
-
-

Notes

Weekly Meal Planner

Day	Breakfast	Lunch	Dinner
Monday			
Tuesday			
Wednesday			
Thursday			
Friday			
Saturday			
Sunday			

Notes

Weekly Meal Planner

things to do

_____

_____

_____

_____

_____

_____

I want healthy dessert

things to buy

_____

_____

_____

_____

_____

_____

List your healthy snacks here . . .

-
-
-
-
-
-

Healthy drinks for this week

-
-
-
-

Notes

Weekly Meal Planner

Day	Breakfast	Lunch	Dinner
Monday			
Tuesday			
Wednesday			
Thursday			
Friday			
Saturday			
Sunday			

Notes

Weekly Meal Planner

things to do

_____
_____
_____
_____
_____
_____
_____

I want healthy dessert

things to buy

_____
_____
_____
_____
_____
_____

List your healthy snacks here . . .

-
-
-
-
-
-

Healthy drinks for this week

-
-
-
-

Notes

Weekly Meal Planner

Day	Breakfast	Lunch	Dinner
Monday			
Tuesday			
Wednesday			
Thursday			
Friday			
Saturday			
Sunday			

Notes

Weekly Meal Planner

things to do

_____

_____

_____

_____

_____

_____

I want healthy dessert

things to buy

_____

_____

_____

_____

_____

_____

List your healthy snacks here . . .

-
-
-
-
-
-
-

Healthy drinks for this week

-
-
-
-

Notes

Weekly Meal Planner

Day	Breakfast	Lunch	Dinner
Monday			
Tuesday			
Wednesday			
Thursday			
Friday			
Saturday			
Sunday			

Notes

Weekly Meal Planner

things to do

I want healthy dessert

_____

_____

_____

_____

_____

_____

_____

things to buy

List your healthy snacks here . . .

Healthy drinks for this week

_____   •

•   _____   •

•   _____   •

•   _____   •

•   _____   •

                   _____   •

Notes

Weekly Meal Planner

Day	Breakfast	Lunch	Dinner
Monday			
Tuesday			
Wednesday			
Thursday			
Friday			
Saturday			
Sunday			

Notes

Weekly Meal Planner

things to do

_____

_____

_____

_____

_____

_____

I want healthy dessert

things to buy

List your healthy snacks here . . .

_____ •

_____ •

_____ •

_____ •

_____ •

_____ •

_____ •

Healthy drinks for this week

•

•

•

•

Notes

Weekly Meal Planner

Day	Breakfast	Lunch	Dinner
Monday			
Tuesday			
Wednesday			
Thursday			
Friday			
Saturday			
Sunday			

Notes

Weekly Meal Planner

things to do

_____

_____

_____

_____

_____

_____

I want healthy dessert

things to buy

List your healthy snacks here . . .

_____

_____

_____

_____

_____

_____

_____

-
-
-
-
-
-

Healthy drinks for this week

-
-
-
-

Notes

Weekly Meal Planner

Day	Breakfast	Lunch	Dinner
Monday			
Tuesday			
Wednesday			
Thursday			
Friday			
Saturday			
Sunday			

Notes

Weekly Meal Planner

things to do

_____
_____
_____
_____
_____

I want healthy dessert

things to buy

_____
_____
_____
_____
_____
_____

List your healthy snacks here . . .

-
-
-
-
-
-

Healthy drinks for this week

-
-
-
-

Notes

Weekly Meal Planner

Day	Breakfast	Lunch	Dinner
Monday			
Tuesday			
Wednesday			
Thursday			
Friday			
Saturday			
Sunday			

Notes

Weekly Meal Planner

things to do

_____
_____
_____
_____
_____

I want healthy dessert

things to buy

_____
_____
_____
_____
_____
_____

List your healthy snacks here . . .

-
-
-
-
-
-
-

Healthy drinks for this week

-
-
-
-

Notes

Weekly Meal Planner

Day	Breakfast	Lunch	Dinner
Monday			
Tuesday			
Wednesday			
Thursday			
Friday			
Saturday			
Sunday			

Notes

Weekly Meal Planner

things to do

_____

_____

_____

_____

_____

_____

I want healthy dessert

things to buy

List your healthy snacks here . . .

Healthy drinks for this week

-
-
-
-

_____

_____

_____

_____

_____

_____

_____

-
-
-
-
-
-
-

Notes

Weekly Meal Planner

Day	Breakfast	Lunch	Dinner
Monday			
Tuesday			
Wednesday			
Thursday			
Friday			
Saturday			
Sunday			

Notes

Weekly Meal Planner

things to do

_____
_____
_____
_____
_____
_____

I want healthy dessert

things to buy

_____
_____
_____
_____
_____
_____

List your healthy snacks here . . .

-
-
-
-
-
-
-

Healthy drinks for this week

-
-
-
-

Notes

Weekly Meal Planner

Day	Breakfast	Lunch	Dinner
Monday			
Tuesday			
Wednesday			
Thursday			
Friday			
Saturday			
Sunday			

Notes

Weekly Meal Planner

things to do

_____

_____

_____

_____

_____

_____

I want healthy dessert

things to buy

_____

_____

_____

_____

_____

_____

List your healthy snacks here . . .

-
-
-
-
-
-
-

Healthy drinks for this week

-
-
-
-

Notes

Weekly Meal Planner

Day	Breakfast	Lunch	Dinner
Monday			
Tuesday			
Wednesday			
Thursday			
Friday			
Saturday			
Sunday			

Notes

Weekly Meal Planner

things to do

_____

_____

_____

_____

_____

_____

I want healthy dessert

things to buy

_____

_____

_____

_____

_____

_____

List your healthy snacks here . . .

-
-
-
-
-
-
-

Healthy drinks for this week

-
-
-
-

Notes

Weekly Meal Planner

Day	Breakfast	Lunch	Dinner
Monday			
Tuesday			
Wednesday			
Thursday			
Friday			
Saturday			
Sunday			

Notes

Weekly Meal Planner

things to do

_____

_____

_____

_____

_____

_____

_____

I want healthy dessert

things to buy

_____

_____

_____

_____

_____

_____

_____

List your healthy snacks here . . .

-
-
-
-
-
-
-

Healthy drinks for this week

-
-
-
-

Notes

Weekly Meal Planner

Day	Breakfast	Lunch	Dinner
Monday			
Tuesday			
Wednesday			
Thursday			
Friday			
Saturday			
Sunday			

Notes

Weekly Meal Planner

things to do

_____
_____
_____
_____
_____
_____
_____

I want healthy dessert

things to buy

_____
_____
_____
_____
_____
_____
_____

List your healthy snacks here . . .

-
-
-
-
-
-
-

Healthy drinks for this week

-
-
-
-

Notes

Weekly Meal Planner

Day	Breakfast	Lunch	Dinner
Monday			
Tuesday			
Wednesday			
Thursday			
Friday			
Saturday			
Sunday			

Notes

Weekly Meal Planner

things to do

_____

_____

_____

_____

_____

_____

I want healthy dessert

things to buy

_____

_____

_____

_____

_____

_____

_____

List your healthy snacks here . . .

-
-
-
-
-
-

Healthy drinks for this week

-
-
-
-

Notes

Weekly Meal Planner

Day	Breakfast	Lunch	Dinner
Monday			
Tuesday			
Wednesday			
Thursday			
Friday			
Saturday			
Sunday			

Notes

Weekly Meal Planner

things to do

_____

_____

_____

_____

_____

_____

I want healthy dessert

things to buy

_____

_____

_____

_____

_____

_____

List your healthy snacks here . . .

-
-
-
-
-
-
-

Healthy drinks for this week

-
-
-
-

Notes

Weekly Meal Planner

Day	Breakfast	Lunch	Dinner
Monday			
Tuesday			
Wednesday			
Thursday			
Friday			
Saturday			
Sunday			

Notes

Weekly Meal Planner

things to do

_____

_____

_____

_____

_____

_____

_____

I want healthy dessert

things to buy

_____

_____

_____

_____

_____

_____

_____

List your healthy snacks here . . .

-
-
-
-
-
-
-

Healthy drinks for this week

-
-
-
-

Notes

Weekly Meal Planner

Day	Breakfast	Lunch	Dinner
Monday			
Tuesday			
Wednesday			
Thursday			
Friday			
Saturday			
Sunday			

Notes

Weekly Meal Planner

things to do

_____
_____
_____

_____

_____

_____

Healthy drinks for this
week

-
-
-
-

I want healthy dessert

things to buy

_____

_____

_____

_____

_____

_____

_____

List your healthy snacks
here . . .

-
-
-
-
-
-
-

Notes

Weekly Meal Planner

Day	Breakfast	Lunch	Dinner
Monday			
Tuesday			
Wednesday			
Thursday			
Friday			
Saturday			
Sunday			

Notes

Weekly Meal Planner

things to do

_____

_____

_____

_____

_____

_____

I want healthy dessert

things to buy

_____

_____

_____

_____

_____

_____

List your healthy snacks here . . .

-
-
-
-
-
-
-

Healthy drinks for this week

-
-
-
-

Notes

Weekly Meal Planner

Day	Breakfast	Lunch	Dinner
Monday			
Tuesday			
Wednesday			
Thursday			
Friday			
Saturday			
Sunday			

Notes

Weekly Meal Planner

things to do

_____

_____

_____

_____

_____

_____

I want healthy dessert

Healthy drinks for this week

-
-
-
-

things to buy

_____

_____

_____

_____

_____

_____

List your healthy snacks here . . .

-
-
-
-
-
-

Notes

Weekly Meal Planner

Day	Breakfast	Lunch	Dinner
Monday			
Tuesday			
Wednesday			
Thursday			
Friday			
Saturday			
Sunday			

Notes

Weekly Meal Planner

things to do

_____

_____

_____

_____

_____

_____

I want healthy dessert

things to buy

_____

_____

_____

_____

_____

_____

List your healthy snacks here . . .

-
-
-
-
-
-
-

Healthy drinks for this week

-
-
-
-

Notes

Weekly Meal Planner

Day	Breakfast	Lunch	Dinner
Monday			
Tuesday			
Wednesday			
Thursday			
Friday			
Saturday			
Sunday			

Notes

Weekly Meal Planner

things to do

_____

_____

_____

_____

_____

_____

_____

I want healthy dessert

things to buy

_____

_____

_____

_____

_____

_____

_____

List your healthy snacks here . . .

-
-
-
-
-
-
-

Healthy drinks for this week

-
-
-
-

Notes

Weekly Meal Planner

Day	Breakfast	Lunch	Dinner
Monday			
Tuesday			
Wednesday			
Thursday			
Friday			
Saturday			
Sunday			

Notes

Weekly Meal Planner

things to do

_____

_____

_____

_____

_____

_____

I want healthy dessert

things to buy

_____

_____

_____

_____

_____

_____

List your healthy snacks here . . .

-
-
-
-
-
-
-

Healthy drinks for this week

-
-
-
-

Notes

Weekly Meal Planner

Day	Breakfast	Lunch	Dinner
Monday			
Tuesday			
Wednesday			
Thursday			
Friday			
Saturday			
Sunday			

Notes

Weekly Meal Planner

things to do

_____

_____

_____

_____

_____

_____

I want healthy dessert

things to buy

_____

_____

_____

_____

_____

_____

_____

List your healthy snacks here . . .

-
-
-
-
-
-
-

Healthy drinks for this week

-
-
-
-

Notes

Weekly Meal Planner

Day	Breakfast	Lunch	Dinner
Monday			
Tuesday			
Wednesday			
Thursday			
Friday			
Saturday			
Sunday			

Notes

Weekly Meal Planner

things to do

_____
_____
_____
_____
_____
_____
_____

I want healthy dessert

things to buy

List your healthy snacks here . . .

Healthy drinks for this week

-
-
-
-

_____
_____
_____
_____
_____
_____
_____

-
-
-
-
-
-
-

Notes

Weekly Meal Planner

Day	Breakfast	Lunch	Dinner
Monday			
Tuesday			
Wednesday			
Thursday			
Friday			
Saturday			
Sunday			

Notes

Weekly Meal Planner

things to do

_____

_____

_____

_____

_____

_____

_____

I want healthy dessert

things to buy

_____

_____

_____

_____

_____

_____

_____

List your healthy snacks here . . .

-
-
-
-
-
-
-

Healthy drinks for this week

-
-
-
-

Notes

Weekly Meal Planner

Day	Breakfast	Lunch	Dinner
Monday			
Tuesday			
Wednesday			
Thursday			
Friday			
Saturday			
Sunday			

Notes

Weekly Meal Planner

things to do

I want healthy dessert

_____

_____

_____

_____

_____

things to buy

List your healthy snacks here . . .

_____
-
_____
-
_____

Healthy drinks for this week

-

_____
-

_____
-

_____
-

_____
-

_____
-

_____
-

Notes

Weekly Meal Planner

Day	Breakfast	Lunch	Dinner
Monday			
Tuesday			
Wednesday			
Thursday			
Friday			
Saturday			
Sunday			

Notes

Weekly Meal Planner

things to do

_____

_____

_____

_____

_____

_____

I want healthy dessert

things to buy

_____

_____

_____

_____

_____

_____

List your healthy snacks here . . .

-
-
-
-
-
-

Healthy drinks for this week

-
-
-
-

Notes

Weekly Meal Planner

Day	Breakfast	Lunch	Dinner
Monday			
Tuesday			
Wednesday			
Thursday			
Friday			
Saturday			
Sunday			

Notes

Weekly Meal Planner

things to do

_____

_____

_____

_____

_____

_____

I want healthy dessert

things to buy

_____

_____

_____

_____

_____

_____

List your healthy snacks here . . .

-
-
-
-
-
-

Healthy drinks for this week

-
-
-
-

Notes

Weekly Meal Planner

Day	Breakfast	Lunch	Dinner
Monday			
Tuesday			
Wednesday			
Thursday			
Friday			
Saturday			
Sunday			

Notes

Weekly Meal Planner

things to do

_____

_____

_____

_____

_____

_____

I want healthy dessert

things to buy

_____

_____

_____

_____

_____

_____

List your healthy snacks here . . .

-
-
-
-
-
-

Healthy drinks for this week

-
-
-
-

Notes

Weekly Meal Planner

Day	Breakfast	Lunch	Dinner
Monday			
Tuesday			
Wednesday			
Thursday			
Friday			
Saturday			
Sunday			

Notes

Weekly Meal Planner

things to do

_____

_____

_____

_____

_____

_____

I want healthy dessert

things to buy

_____

_____

_____

_____

_____

_____

List your healthy snacks here . . .

-
-
-
-
-
-
-

Healthy drinks for this week

-
-
-
-

Notes

Weekly Meal Planner

Day	Breakfast	Lunch	Dinner
Monday			
Tuesday			
Wednesday			
Thursday			
Friday			
Saturday			
Sunday			

Notes

Weekly Meal Planner

things to do

_____

_____

_____

_____

_____

_____

_____

I want healthy dessert

things to buy

_____

_____

_____

_____

_____

_____

List your healthy snacks here . . .

-
-
-
-
-
-

Healthy drinks for this week

-
-
-
-

Notes

Weekly Meal Planner

Day	Breakfast	Lunch	Dinner
Monday			
Tuesday			
Wednesday			
Thursday			
Friday			
Saturday			
Sunday			

Notes

Weekly Meal Planner

things to do

_____

_____

_____

_____

_____

_____

I want healthy dessert

things to buy

List your healthy snacks here . . .

_____

_____

_____

_____

_____

_____

-
-
-
-
-
-
-

Healthy drinks for this week

-
-
-
-

Notes

Weekly Meal Planner

Day	Breakfast	Lunch	Dinner
Monday			
Tuesday			
Wednesday			
Thursday			
Friday			
Saturday			
Sunday			

Notes

Weekly Meal Planner

things to do

_____

_____

_____

_____

_____

_____

I want healthy dessert

things to buy

_____

_____

_____

_____

_____

_____

List your healthy snacks here . . .

-
-
-
-
-
-
-

Healthy drinks for this week

-
-
-
-

Notes

Weekly Meal Planner

Day	Breakfast	Lunch	Dinner
Monday			
Tuesday			
Wednesday			
Thursday			
Friday			
Saturday			
Sunday			

Notes

Weekly Meal Planner

things to do

_____

_____

_____

_____

_____

_____

I want healthy dessert

things to buy

_____

_____

_____

_____

_____

_____

List your healthy snacks here . . .

-
-
-
-
-
-
-

Healthy drinks for this week

-
-
-
-

Notes

Weekly Meal Planner

Day	Breakfast	Lunch	Dinner
Monday			
Tuesday			
Wednesday			
Thursday			
Friday			
Saturday			
Sunday			

Notes

Weekly Meal Planner

things to do

_____

_____

_____

_____

_____

_____

_____

I want healthy dessert

things to buy

_____

_____

_____

_____

_____

_____

_____

List your healthy snacks here . . .

-
-
-
-
-
-
-

Healthy drinks for this week

-
-
-
-

Notes

Weekly Meal Planner

Day	Breakfast	Lunch	Dinner
Monday			
Tuesday			
Wednesday			
Thursday			
Friday			
Saturday			
Sunday			

Notes

Weekly Meal Planner

things to do

_____

_____

_____

_____

_____

_____

I want healthy dessert

things to buy

_____

_____

_____

_____

_____

_____

_____

List your healthy snacks here . . .

-
-
-
-
-
-
-

Healthy drinks for this week

-
-
-
-

Notes

Weekly Meal Planner

Day	Breakfast	Lunch	Dinner
Monday			
Tuesday			
Wednesday			
Thursday			
Friday			
Saturday			
Sunday			

Notes

Weekly Meal Planner

things to do

_____
_____
_____
_____
_____
_____
_____

I want healthy dessert

Healthy drinks for this week

-
-
-
-

things to buy

_____
_____
_____
_____
_____
_____
_____

List your healthy snacks here . . .

-
-
-
-
-
-
-

Notes

Weekly Meal Planner

Day	Breakfast	Lunch	Dinner
Monday			
Tuesday			
Wednesday			
Thursday			
Friday			
Saturday			
Sunday			

Notes

Weekly Meal Planner

things to do

I want healthy dessert

_____

_____

_____

_____

_____

_____

Healthy drinks for this week

things to buy

List your healthy snacks here . . .

-
-
-
-

_____

_____

_____

_____

_____

_____

_____

-
-
-
-
-
-
-

Notes

Weekly Meal Planner

Day	Breakfast	Lunch	Dinner
Monday			
Tuesday			
Wednesday			
Thursday			
Friday			
Saturday			
Sunday			

Notes

Weekly Meal Planner

things to do

_____

_____

_____

_____

_____

_____

I want healthy dessert

things to buy

_____

_____

_____

_____

_____

_____

List your healthy snacks here . . .

-
-
-
-
-
-
-

Healthy drinks for this week

-
-
-
-

Notes

Weekly Meal Planner

Day	Breakfast	Lunch	Dinner
Monday			
Tuesday			
Wednesday			
Thursday			
Friday			
Saturday			
Sunday			

Notes

Weekly Meal Planner

things to do

_____

_____

_____

_____

_____

_____

I want healthy dessert

things to buy

_____

_____

_____

_____

_____

_____

_____

List your healthy snacks here . . .

-
-
-
-
-
-
-

Healthy drinks for this week

-
-
-
-

Notes

Weekly Meal Planner

Day	Breakfast	Lunch	Dinner
Monday			
Tuesday			
Wednesday			
Thursday			
Friday			
Saturday			
Sunday			

Notes

Weekly Meal Planner

things to do

I want healthy dessert

_____

_____

_____

_____

_____

_____

things to buy

List your healthy snacks here . . .

_____
_____
_____
_____
_____
_____
_____

-
-
-
-
-
-

Healthy drinks for this week

-
-
-
-

Notes

Weekly Meal Planner

Day	Breakfast	Lunch	Dinner
Monday			
Tuesday			
Wednesday			
Thursday			
Friday			
Saturday			
Sunday			

Notes

Weekly Meal Planner

things to do

_____

_____

_____

_____

_____

_____

_____

I want healthy dessert

things to buy

_____

_____

_____

_____

_____

_____

_____

List your healthy snacks here . . .

-
-
-
-
-
-
-

Healthy drinks for this week

-
-
-
-

Notes

* 9 7 8 1 6 8 3 2 1 8 5 1 7 *